World's Greatest
LEADERS

Wonder
House

(An imprint of Prakash Books)

(An imprint of Prakash Books)

contact@wonderhousebooks.com

ISBN : 9789388369046

CONTENTS

ABRAHAM LINCOLN

BIRTH: *February 12, 1809*
Hodgenville, Kentucky, USA

DEATH: *April 15, 1865 (aged 56)*
Washington, D.C., USA

Abraham Lincoln was the most influential president of America. He led the country during the American Civil War. He was fondly called "Honest Abe" and "Father Abraham".

Abraham Lincoln was born on February 12, 1809, in Kentucky to Thomas Lincoln and Nancy Lincoln. From a very young age, Lincoln took a keen interest in studies. For the most part, he was self-educated. Even though both his parents were illiterate and unschooled, they wanted the best for him.

To support his family, Lincoln worked many odd jobs such as being a shopkeeper and a postmaster. Later, he moved to politics. And at the age of 25, he won a seat in the Illinois legislature. One of the main reasons Lincoln entered politics was because he was against slavery, which had spread to different regions of the US. He wanted to develop and expand the United States. His main focus was on commerce rather than agriculture.

Before Lincoln became president, he served in the Illinois state legislature for many terms. To understand the political ground, he studied law and successfully passed the bar examination in 1836. Later, he worked as a lawyer under John T. Stuart. There, he earned the name 'Honest Abe'. In 1846, he competed for a seat in the US Congress, which he won. Lincoln served as a congressman for one whole term. For his next election, he delivered a speech in Peoria in which he addressed his abhorrence for slavery and talked about the equality of rights amongst people.

For his candidacy, he spoke about the anti-slavery and Free Soil ideologies. In 1858, Lincoln was chosen for the US Senate. During this time began the famous Lincoln-Douglas debates, also known as 'The Great Debates of 1858'. It was a series of seven debates against the Democrat Stephen Douglas, mostly revolving around the issue of slavery.

The year 1860 was quite a prosperous year for Lincoln. He fought for the seat of the president of the United States.

Lincoln finally won the 1860 elections and became the president in 1861. He gained lots of support from the North and the West. But at that time, Southern states did not want Lincoln to be the president. They were against his policies. The South decided to remove itself from the Union and formed a separate nation called the Confederate States of America.

Lincoln refused to accept the Confederacy and declared it illegal. He still stood strongly for free-soil and slave-free states. This situation created the most deadly conflict in America's history. In 1861, the Civil War started, just a month after Lincoln joined office.

He took the help of the Northern state armies to defeat the South. It soon turned into a bloody war which lasted for four years and millions of Americans lost their lives. But, Lincoln still managed to hold the country together.

In 1863, he announced the Emancipation Proclamation, an order that freed the slaves in the Confederate states. It also created a thirteenth Amendment, which released all slaves in the United States in the following years. Lincoln spent months preparing the army and the country for emancipation. In a short time, around three million slaves were released from the Confederate regions. Those slaves were then absorbed into the military according to the policy that Lincoln had established.

On April 9, 1865, the Civil War finally ended. During the war, many Southern states were heavily damaged. Lincoln wanted to help these states but, sadly, he did not live long enough to see the country rebuild itself.

Lincoln married Mary Todd on November 4, 1842. The couple had four sons. Lincoln was assassinated by John Wilkes Booth while he was watching a play. He died on April 15, 1865, at the age of 56. Post death, his body was wrapped in the American flag.

BARACK OBAMA

BIRTH: August 4, 1961
Honolulu, Hawaii, USA

Barack Obama is an ex-politician, attorney and author and the first African-American president of the United States of America. He served as the 44th president, from 2009 to 2017. Prior to that, he was a constitutional law professor, civil rights lawyer, and state senator. Obama, as a president, was the mastermind behind a plethora of significant pieces of legislation, notably the American Recovery and Reinvestment Act of 2009, and the Affordable Care Unit Act, popularly known as 'Obamacare'.

Barack Hussein Obama was born on August 4, 1961 in Hawaii to Barack Obama, Sr. and Ann Dunham. His father was an economist and his mother was an anthropologist. The couple separated in 1964 and Obama, Sr. returned to Kenya, his native country. Obama, with his mother, shifted to Jakarta in 1967. Ann had to travel for work, and so, at the age of 10, Obama was sent to Hawaii to live with his grandparents. After school, Obama joined Occidental College. He gave his first public speech there, for which he was highly appreciated. In 1981, Obama transferred to Columbia University and graduated with a degree in English literature and political science. In 1988, Obama took admission at Harvard Law School, where he became the first black president of the Harvard Law Review.

After graduating from Harvard, Obama worked at Business International Corporation. Later, he took up a job at the New York Public Interest Research Group, a non-partisan political organization. While working, Obama wrote his memoir, Dreams of My Father, which was highly appreciated by readers and critics alike.

During the next twelve years, Obama worked as a community organizer and a teacher of constitutional law at the University of Chicago Law School. In 1997, Obama started his political career as a member of the Illinois state senate. He supported bipartite efforts to improve healthcare and increase tax credits for children. Due to his diligence and hard work, he was re-elected to the state senate. In 2005, Obama became a US Senator. As a senator, Obama sponsored legislation to support victims of Hurricane Katrina, ensure the safety of consumer products, and reduce the incidence of homelessness among veterans.

During the same time, he wrote his second book, The Audacity of Hope, which also became a New York Times bestseller.

In 2007, Obama stood against Hilary Clinton in the Democratic Party presidential primaries. Obama won this primary race and made ending the Iraq War and passing healthcare reform his primary campaign issues. He then won the presidential election against John McCain with 365 electoral votes and 52% of the popular vote.

Within his first 100 days as the president, Obama launched the American Recovery and Reinvestment Act of 2009, a legislation designed to address and mitigate the worst effects of the great recession of 2008. Under the Recovery Act, vast sums of money were injected into the economy via tax incentives, incentives for infrastructure development, scientific research, and aid for low-income workers. Leading economists agreed that the initiative reduced the level of unemployment and was an aid in helping the economy grow.

In March 2010, Obama designed the Patient Protection and Affordable Care Act. It was initiated to ensure that every American could get health insurance at subsidized prices. On May 11, 2011, Obama successfully commanded Operation Neptune Spear, in Pakistan, which sought to kill Osama Bin Laden.

In 2012, Obama stood for re-election, center-ing the campaign around social issues, notably, health care and social security. In November 2012, Obama defeated his main opponent, Mitt Romney. In his second term, Obama initiated negotiations with Iran, which eventually led to a nuclear deal with the Middle Eastern country. In 2012, Obama signed several executive orders to reduce gun violence, especially after the mass shooting at the Sandy Hook Elementary School in December 2012. At the White House, Obama said "If there is even one thing we can do to reduce this violence, if there is even one life that can be saved, then we've got an obligation to try."

On October 3, 1992, Obama got married to Michelle LaVaughn Robinson. They have two daughters, Malia and Sasha Obama. Barack Obama was a people's president. Hundreds of thousands came to witness his re-election to the president's office. The true impact and significance of his presidency will be understood, in its entirety, in the years to come.

CHARLES DE GAULLE

BIRTH: *November 22, 1890*
Lille, France

DEATH: *November 9, 1970 (aged 79)*
Colombey-les-Deux-Églises, France

Charles de Gaulle was a French army officer and political leader who led the French resistance in World War II against Nazi Germany. He was also the chairperson of the Provisional Government of the French Republic.

Charles de Gaulle was born on November 22, 1890 to Henri de Gaulle and Jeanne Maillot de Gaulle. He grew up in Lille, France with four siblings. With an aspiration to become a military leader, de Gaulle's parents enrolled him in a military academy named Saint Cyr in 1909. He performed exceptionally well at the institute and attained the thirteenth position amongst 210 cadets who were enrolled there. He graduated from Saint Cyr in 1912.

He soon joined the 33rd Infantry Regiment and shifted to France's Arras region. During this time, the French soldiers were busy preparing for World War I. De Gaulle devised new and better strategies for battle by consulting with the senior officers at Arras. De Gaulle and some other soldiers were sent to Dinant, a Belgian town, to keep the German army at bay. He came back from the battle wounded by a bullet.

In 1916, de Gaulle fought in the Battle of Verdun. From 1919-21, Poland and Russia were fighting a war during which De Gaulle became a part of the French Military Mission. He tried to guide the Polish troops by serving their chief instructor. De Gaulle also became the commander of a light infantry battalion in the

1920s, and traveled to Rhineland and Syria for different tasks.

While de Gaulle was held by the German military, he wrote a book named *The Enemy's House Divided*. The book discussed the operations and functions of the German Empire. It was published in 1924. In 1934, he penned another book, *Vers l'armée de métier*, in which he talked about how to organize the army professionally.

In 1930, de Gaulle was stationed at France and promoted to the position of lieutenant colonel. His innovative military strategies became a major highlight of the Second World War. Under his leadership, the troops were able to restrict the violent German forces to the Caumont region. At the same time, Prime Minister Paul Reynaud promoted him to position of the under-secretary for national defense and war.

In 1940, de Gaulle and his military colleagues were infuriated by Marshal Pétain's decision to negotiate terms with Nazi Germany, and started a rebellion against the government. He created the Free French Forces for those French natives who resided outside France, like himself. In 1941, de Gaulle founded the Free French National Council and became its president. Thus, when elections were held in 1945, De Gaulle gained the support of French nationals and was elected as the president of France. However, he resigned from the position because of conflicts with the Communist party.

De Gaulle regained the position in 1958 and became the eighteenth president of France. As soon as he returned to power, de Gaulle undertook the task of putting an end to violence in one of the French colonies, Algeria. Soon, Algeria became a free nation. De Gaulle served France as the president for eleven years and had to step down from the position in 1969 due to a revolt carried out by some students.

In 1945, de Gaulle was awarded the Grand Croix of the Legion d'Honneur for his brilliant strategies as a military leader. In the same year, he was honored with the Chief Commander of the US Legion of Merit award and Grand Cross of the Order of the Dragon of Annam award. He also received the Grand Collar of the Order of the Pahlavi of Iran and Grand Cordon of the Order of the Two Rivers of Iraq. Apart from this, he received medals like the Medal of the Rancagua of Chile and the Medal of Mexico.

Charles de Gaulle got married to Yvonne Vendroux on April 7, 1921. The couple became parents of three children named Anne, Elisabeth, and Phillippe. Unfortunately, Anne died at the age of twenty due to pneumonia.

De Gaulle passed away on November 9, 1970 at the age of eighty. It's believed that he breathed his last when he was watching television on the evening of 9th November. The doctors discovered later that de Gaulle had died due to ruptured blood vessels.

CHE GUEVARA

BIRTH: *June 14, 1928*
Rosario, Santa Fe, Argentina

DEATH: *October 9, 1967*
La Higuera, Vallegrande, Bolivia

Che Guevara was a legendary political activist, doctor, author, guerrilla leader, diplomat and military theorist. He gave his life to the downfall of imperialism and the establishment of socialism. Che Guevara was listed in *Time* magazine's list of '100 most influential people of the 20th century'. For his hard work and perseverance, Che Guevara became the counter-cultural symbol of revolution and rebellion.

Che Guevara was the eldest son of Ernesto Guevara Lynch and Celia De La Serna y Liosa. He was introduced to political perspectives and realities, primarily leftism, which left a great impact on the revolutionary from a very young age. He soon developed an affinity for reading, especially about revolutionaries and leaders like Jawaharlal Nehru, Emilio Salgari, Karl Marx and William Faulkner.

However, Guevara learned about the prevailing economic conditions and poor adversities only after going for two of the longest journeys of his life: a 4500-km long journey on a bicycle through the rural province of Northern Argentina in 1950, and a nine-month long, 8000-km journey on a motorcycle through most of South America in 1951. The notes taken on both the journeys were compiled into a book titled *The Motorcycle Diaries*.

After studying medicine and graduating from Buenos Aires University in 1953, he undertook another journey which further affirmed his views against capitalism and created within him an urge to save the world from misery.

At the same time, he worked at the General Hospital in Mexico, took lectures in the University of Mexico on medicine, and became a part-time photographer for a news agency.

In 1955, he was introduced to Fidel Castro, a revolutionary leader. Guevara instantly joined hands with him to fight against poverty and the exploitation of the poor. Later, Guevara helped Castro fight against the Batista regime in Cuba.

In 1956, Guevara and Castro came up with the 26th of July Movement, a revolutionary organization, and aimed to set up their base in the Sierra Maestra mountains. However, after an attack by the government troops, only 22 people of the original 82 were left. Soon after, they attacked military camps and built their stock of weapons. They ultimately gained control over the territory. Guevara and Castro distributed the land equally amongst the peasants and in return the peasants helped them fight against the Batista forces.

Looking at the increasing popularity of Castro's army, the government started publicly executing people. This created tension between the government and the guerrilla forces. By 1958, Castro's army, comprising only the poor and deprived, received support from the middle-class and wealthy families, primarily doctors, lawyers, accountants and social workers. Castro's troops soon defeated the military.

Along with other important fights against the military and government, Castro's army took over Havana on January 8, 1959. Soon, Guevara became the commander of La Cabana Fortress prison and was to institute revolutionary justice against those who were considered war criminals and traitors.

In June 1959, Guevara went to Singapore, Hong Kong and other Bandung Pact countries. After his three-month long trip, he was made the minister of industries. During his tenure as a minister, he confiscated the land owned by the US Government and re-distributed the same amongst its real owners.

He also emphasized the importance of literacy. Guevara mainly focused on educating trainers, who would transform the illiterate population into a literate one. Guevara also set up educational institutes in rural areas. During his tenure, the literacy rate went up from 60% to 96%.

Later, he was made the finance minister, and president of the National Bank. He focused on balancing the social system and eliminating inequality. In addition, he also provided health care, housing and employment facilities to the people of Cuba.

Guevara got married to Hilda Gadea in 1955. However, they soon separated. In June 1959, Guevara married Aleida March and was blessed with four children.

Soon after, his efforts to create an uprising in Bolivia backfired and the Bolivian President captured Guevara and sentenced him to death. Che Guevara was killed on October 9, 1967. His body was found four years later, near a Vallegrande airstrip. His remains were laid at rest with military honors in a mausoleum in Santa Clara, Cuba.

DENG XIAOPING

BIRTH: August 22, 1904
Guang'an, Sichuan, China

DEATH: February 19, 1997
Beijing, China

Deng Xiaoping is remembered as a paramount leader and reformist of the people's Republic of China. He led the country to domestic stability and economic growth after the damaging excesses of the Cultural Revolution. Though he never took office as the head of government or state, Xiaoping is known for developing China into one of the fastest growing economies of the world.

Born to Deng Wenming and Dan, Deng Xiaoping was the youngest of seven siblings. His father Deng Wenming was a middle-class landlord. Deng graduated from Chongqing Preparatory School in 1919.

Xiaoping went to France in the 1920s, but focused more on his jobs rather than his studies. He met Zhou Enlai there, who changed his life. Xiaoping took an interest in politics, especially in Marxism. In 1920, he joined the Chinese Communist Youth League in Europe. By 1924, he became a crucial member of the General Branch of Youth League. In 1922, he moved to the Soviet Union to enroll at the Moscow Sun Yat-sen University.

Fleeing from China after an unsuccessful attempt to resolve the split of Nationalist and Communist parties, Xiaoping settled in Wuhan and became an important leader and politician there. Soon, he shifted to Shanghai where he lived till 1929. He was responsible for organizing protests which resulted in serious casualties and forced people to leave the party. This helped Xiaoping rise amongst the ranks.

He was absorbed under the leadership of Mao Zedong, who had a great impact on Xiaoping. Soon after, Xiaoping became the director of the propaganda department. Later, Xiaoping moved to Chongqing to negotiate between the Nationalists and Communists, but it was in vain. While Chiang Kai-shek established his government in Nanjing, Xiaoping strengthened his base in the rural areas.

The same year, Xiaoping and Mao's party defeated Chiang Kai-shek's government and established the People's Republic of China. After a long struggle, Xiaoping was posted in the Southwest Bureau as the first secretary on October 1, 1949. After completing his tenure, Xiaoping was relocated to Beijing, where he took up various positions in the government. In four years, Xiaoping became the secretary general of the CPC Central Committee and vice chairman of the Central Military Commission.

In 1957, he was appointed as the secretary general of the Secretariat. But soon, due to the economic conditions under Mao's government his supporters dwindled. Mao's leadership was under question and soon he was replaced by Xiaoping.

Along with Liu Shaoqi, Xiaoping promoted economical, foreign and domestic policies, which didn't go well with Mao's egalitarian policies as they stressed on self-interest. After the death of Mao in 1976, Xiaoping became the 'paramount leader' of the Communist Party.

Through his powerful post, Xiaoping brought about several political, cultural, and economic reforms. All his reforms emphasized on material incentives and individual responsibility. Besides, he urged the formation of skilled labor for economic growth and development. In addition, he decentralized a few industries and small-scale businesses to achieve better growth. Farmers were given individual control of profit and production. In fact, this change resulted in a significant increase in the production.

Regarding foreign exchange, Xiaoping brought about a huge difference in cultural ties with other countries. He strengthened cultural ties with the Western countries and opened Chinese enterprise to foreign investment.

However, his dominance ended when he stepped down from his post in the CCP's Central Committee. He withdrew himself from the political scene in 1992.

Deng Xiaoping married thrice in his lifetime. His first wife died while giving birth to their child, who also died. In 1933, his second wife, Jin Weiying, abandoned him. At last, he married Zhuo Lin in 1939, with whom he had five children. On February 19, 1997, Xiaoping took his last breath. He died of Parkinson's disease and lung infection. After his death, his organs were donated for medical research.

Xiaoping was the only Chinese politician and leader whose statues and memorials were constructed, in his honor, during his lifetime.

FIDEL CASTRO

BIRTH: *August 13, 1926*
Biran, Cuba

DEATH: *November 25, 2016 (aged 90)*
Havana, Cuba

Fidel Castro was the most famous communist leader in history. He successfully developed his country into the first communist state in the western hemisphere. He was an influential prime minister, president and commander-in-chief of Cuba.

Fidel Alejandro Castro Ruz was born on August 13, 1926 near Biran, Cuba to Angel Castro y Argiz and Lina Ruz Gonzalez. As a child,

Fidel attended many schools. He went to Jesuit boarding schools and did well academically. But he was more interested in sports; he played for the school's baseball team. Fidel continued his studies and went to the University of Havana to study law.

His time as a law student helped him to develop an interest in politics and governance. He protested against the corrupt government of his time. He also joined the University Committee for the Independence of Puerto Rico. The committee was against invasion by the USA, in the Caribbean. He also fought for the independence of Puerto Rico. By the time he completed his graduation, he had made a significant difference. Castro graduated in 1950 and soon opened a law office.

For the next two years, Castro fought to be a part of Cuba's House of Representatives. But the government canceled the elections. Castro started a revolution. Castro and his brother, Raul, wanted to take control of the government. But their plan did not work, and they were both sent to prison. Two years later, Castro was freed from prison.

Castro moved to Mexico and prepared for his next revolution. He met a fellow revolutionary Che Guevara, who became an important figure in Castro's revolution. In 1956, Castro and Guevara took a small army to Cuba. They sailed on a yacht named *Granma* to the eastern coast of Cuba. But the Batista government forces surrounded them. Castro, his brother Raul, and Guevara, escaped deep into the south-eastern Cuban mountain range. They had no weapons or stock. Still, they fought in a guerrilla war against Batista. Eventually, Castro, with his army, defeated Batista's government on January 1, 1959.

Castro returned to Havana and became the prime minister. In 1959, Castro was declared the leader of Cuba. He ruled for almost fifty years. He followed Marxism. Castro created a new government for Cuba. He controlled all US-owned businesses such as the oil refineries and factories. His plan was successful, and it ended diplomatic relations with the United States. Freedom of speech and the press was restricted and a trade limitation was imposed which still stands today.

When Castro came to power, he ended all legal discrimination in the country. He provided electricity in the countryside and gave full employment to his people. He also promoted education and healthcare. Castro built new schools and medical facilities. Despite this, many people opposed his rule in Cuba. The situation got worse, which forced Castro to flee the country.

In 1961, many exiled militants invaded Cuba at the Bay of Pigs. Their main motive was to oust the Castro government. The Bay of Pigs invasion started when President John F. Kennedy ordered the overthrow of Castro. Castro skilfully handled the situation, even though it was a surprise attack. Castro's military subdued the rebels. The invasion was a disaster and many of them were killed.

Around 1976, Castro became president.

But his health started deteriorating. In 2008, he permanently resigned. He gave the presidency of Cuba to his brother Raul. After his retirement, he began to write a column called *Reflections of Fidel*. He shared his personal experiences and opinions in the column.

For all his revolutionary work, Castro received the Order of Lenin. He was the first foreigner to be honored with this award thrice. Castro was very much against racism. He was awarded South Africa's highest civilian award for foreigners, called the Order of Good Hope. Throughout his life, he was acknowledged by governments and offices around the world.

Castro married Mirta Diaz Balart in 1948. His marriage with Balart exposed him to the elite Cuban lifestyle. But the marriage didn't last very long. He was also the father of eleven children. Castro died on November 25, 2016, at the age of ninety, in Cuba.

FRANKLIN D. ROOSEVELT

BIRTH: January 30, 1882
Hyde Park, New York, USA

DEATH: April 12, 1945
Warm Springs, Georgia, USA

The 32nd President of the United States, Franklin Roosevelt was a key figure of the twentieth century. A man with a vision, he led the United States in its worst crisis and helped the country to rise against the Great Depression.

Franklin Delano Roosevelt was born on January 30, 1882 to James Roosevelt I and Sara Ann

Delano. Franklin belonged to a wealthy family and was brought up in a privileged atmosphere. He finished his preliminary education from Groton School, and later enrolled in Harvard University, from where he graduated in 1903.

Roosevelt entered the New York Senate in 1910 with the help of his family's reputation and wealth. The first episode that helped establish his political legacy was when he opposed Tammany Hall, an organization that was the political machine of Democratic party. As the chairman of the agriculture committee, Roosevelt brought new reforms that supported social welfare and labor programs for women and children.

In 1912, Roosevelt supported Woodrow Wilson in the presidential elections. He successfully got himself appointed as the administrator in Wilson's team. However, in 1913, Roosevelt resigned from his post and accepted the position of assistant secretary of the navy.

He spent seven years in the job and understood its intricacies. In the navy, he devoted himself to building a large and efficient naval force for the country and worked on financial plans for its smooth functioning.

In 1921, Roosevelt was diagnosed with polio due to which his lower body became paralyzed. People believed that this would be the end of his political career. However, Roosevelt conquered his disease.

During the 1920s, Roosevelt worked on his relationship with the Democratic Party. He supported Al Smith for the chair of the governor. Finally, in 1928, Roosevelt replaced Smith and won the seat of governor, which he held until 1932.

In 1932, he stood in the presidential elections against the Republican Party during the Great Depression. Soon after, Roosevelt won the elections aided by his charming mannerisms, optimistic outlook and buoyant spirit. Roosevelt promised to provide relief, recovery and reform to the public and its economy. He also advocated dismantling useless commissions and reducing public expenditure.

During Roosevelt's presidency, the country was going through a major crisis. The rate of unemployment was high, the agricultural crisis was still going on, and industrial production was at rock bottom.

True to his words, Roosevelt jumped straight into action and introduced new economic policies called the New Deal. His agencies took care of agricultural administration and farm prices; civilian conservation corporations employed youth; the wages and prices of production were kept in check; and the banks took care of the stock exchange and subsidized mortgages.

While working with Republican Senator George Norris, Roosevelt created the largest government–owned industrial enterprise in American history. Roosevelt also introduced the Second New Deal in 1935 where he formed the Works Progress Administration to set up national relief agencies.

In 1936, he again received maximum votes and was elected as the president of the country. In 1940, Roosevelt won a third term as the president of the United States. Roosevelt started suffering from major health issues like high blood pressure and atherosclerosis. In 1944, Roosevelt once again won the elections and was chosen as the president for the fourth term.

Franklin Roosevelt married Eleanor Roosevelt in 1905. The couple had six children. Roosevelt passed away on April 12, 1945, after suffering a massive cerebral hemorrhage. The next day, his body was placed in a flag-draped coffin and buried in the Rose Garden of his Springwood Estate in Hyde Park, New York.

Franklin Roosevelt was one of the most be-loved presidents of the United States. To describe Roosevelt, Jean Edward Smith said, "He lifted himself from a wheelchair to lift the nation from its knees." He was the only president of the United States to be elected for four terms.

GAMAL ABDEL NASSER

BIRTH: *January 15, 1918*
Alexandria, Egypt

DEATH: *September 28, 1970*
Cairo, Egypt

G amal Abdel Nasser was the second president of Egypt. He served from 1956 until his death in 1970. Gamal Abdel Nasser replaced the monarchy with a new government. Though he is reputed as a controversial man, he remains one of the most influential figures in the history of the Arab world.

Gamal Abdel Nasser was born to Fahima and

Abdel Nasser Hussain in Bakos, Alexandria. In 1926, Gamal lost his mother, which plunged him into severe depression. Gamal completed his secondary schooling from Ras el-Tin Secondary School. He was involved in political events. In the following years, he organized many anti-British street demonstrations where he strongly protested against the Anglo-Egyptian Treaty of 1936.

In 1938, Nasser graduated from the Royal Military Academy as a second lieutenant. His first battlefield was during the 1948 war in Palestine. Gamal provided his services to the military as a teacher and an officer. Post war, Gamal became an instructor in the military, and at the same time, formed a nationalist group of young militants who strongly supported revolution. Later, with the same group, he formed a free association for officers. His main aim was to overthrow the British, and the Egyptian royal family. He was soon elected as the chairman of the organization.

Around 1952, the number of members in the group rose to ninety. On June 18, 1953,

Egypt was declared a republic. Major General Muhammed Naguib served as the president while Ali Maher retained his position as the prime minister. A revolutionary command council was formed in which Naguib served as the chairman. However, Maher did not agree with many of the reforms and policies proposed by Naguib, so he resigned from the post in the same year.

In 1953, Nasser deposed Naguib from the post and put him under house arrest. Nasser soon emerged as the prime minister and chairman of the RCC. Because of protests from the Muslim Brotherhood, Nasser released Naguib from house arrest, but did not give him his post back.

Following these protests, Nasser was barely able to save himself from assassination attempts. He ordered house arrests for thousands of members of the Brotherhood and those loyal to Naguib. Nasser soon became the unquestionable leader of Egypt.

In 1956, Nasser formed a new constitution under which Egypt became a one-party political system. Soon, Islam was declared as the official religion of the country. Nasser gained the support of a majority of Egyptians.

With Nasser as the president of the country, Egypt's economy saw growth. Nasser also got monetary support from the US and Britain. While Nasser continuously vouched for Arab independence from the British, he developed cordial relations with the Soviet Union. The US and UK thus withdrew their financial aid.

The British prime minister, scared of Nasser nationalizing and cutting off oil supplies, formed a secret society with France and Israel, and planned an attack on Egypt. On October 29, 1956, the Israeli Army invaded Egypt and two days later, British and French armies bombed Egyptian airfields. However, by March 1957, all the forces retreated and the prisoners of war were released.

Nasser reaffirmed his position as the president of the country. Later that year, Nasser ensur-ed increased agricultural production and a greater investment in industrialization. In fact, it was under his rule that Egypt's middle class took important political decisions and economic positions. Women were also offered more freedom.

In 1962, Nasser adopted socialism. He introduced the National Charter and a new constitution, which also highlighted universal health care, vocational schooling, affordable housing, women's rights, and family planning.

Nasser was re-elected to the post of the president. However, in 1967, during the Arab-Israeli War, also known as the Six Day War, Egypt faced a lot of destruction. Following this, Nasser tried to resign from his post, but was forced to continue. In 1970, the US sponsored the Roger's Plan and the Israelis retreated.

Nasser married Tahia Kazem in 1944; they had five children. Nasser died on September 28, 1970, due to a major heart attack. He was buried at Nasir Mosque, which was later renamed the Abdel Nasser Mosque.

GEORGE WASHINGTON

BIRTH: *February 22, 1732*
Westmoreland, Virginia, USA

DEATH: *December 14, 1799 (aged 67)*
Mount Vernon, Virginia, USA

George Washington was the first president of the United States and commander-in-chief of the Continental Army during the American Revolution. He was one of the Founding Fathers of the United States.

George Washington was born on February 22, 1732, in Westmoreland, Virginia to Augustine Washington and Mary Ball Washington.

His father was a landowner and plantation owner, due to which George spent most of his childhood on the farm. He lost his father when he was only eleven. He managed the plantation with his mother and supported his family. George was taught at home by private tutors. After the death of his father, his half-brother, Lawrence Washington became his guardian.

George had an interest in mathematics as a child which helped him to become a surveyor. He completed his formal schooling at the age of fifteen. At the age of sixteen, George started working as a surveyor. He took measurements of new lands and mapped them out in detail. He was also a part of a professional survey team, arranged by William Fairfax, a relative. Because of his work, he traveled a lot and moved to Virginia. His journey into the Virginia forest earned him enough money, with which he acquired land of his own. In 1749, he got a surveyor's license from the College of William and Mary.

By 1750s, the French had started to expand their territory. In 1753, Virginia's lieutenant governor, Robert Dinwiddie, sent Washington to Fort LeBoeuf, which is now located in Waterford, Pennsylvania. Washington was given the task to ask the French to leave the area as it was claimed by the British. He successfully did this job. A few years later, Washington became a leader of the Virginia army, although he had no prior experience in the military. He was also included in the French and Indian wars.

In 1759, Washington resigned from his job and returned to Mount Vernon. It was a fruitful time for Washington. He expanded his brother's property in Mount Vernon. He even grew different types of crops such as wheat and corn, fruit orchards and fishery. Washington continuously experimented with new crops and techniques of land conservation.

Later, he was selected to the Virginia House of Burgesses where he served until 1774. The next year, Washington became the commander-in-chief of the Continental Army. The British in Boston attacked the area and a war broke out. The war lasted for eight long years, but Washington proved to be a great general. Throughout the war, he motivated his ill-trained and ill-equipped troops. His army mostly consisted of farmers. Washington's army of farmers fought against trained British soldiers. His army eventually gained a victory over the British. One of their most courageous feats was the crossing of the Delaware River on Christmas, leading to the ultimate victory at Yorktown, Virginia. The British Army was defeated at Yorktown in 1781. After the war ended, Washington became a national hero.

Washington remained commander-in-chief until the Treaty of Paris was signed in 1783. It satisfied the under-paid Continental Army. With this treaty, Washington wanted the Continental Congress to pay proper compensation to army people. After the conflicts were resolved, Washington resumed the life of a plantation owner. But he also continued to be involved in national politics.

In 1789, Washington was selected as the first president of the United States. He served as president for two terms, and it was a peaceful time for the country. He established the duties of future presidents and also the traditions of the office of the president of the United States which continue to stand today. He played a significant role in building the Constitution. He also established the first presidential cabinet during his term. The cabinet included his friends Thomas Jefferson, secretary of state, and Alexander Hamilton, secretary of the treasury. He remained president for eight years. However, Washington felt that the country needed a president who was not too powerful and would not rule like a king over many years.

Washington married Martha Dandridge, a widow with two children in 1759. Washington died on December 14, 1799 in his home at Mount Vernon, after he suffered from a bad cold and throat infection. He left a lasting legacy as the 'Father of the Country'. He has one of the most enduring legacies of any American in history.

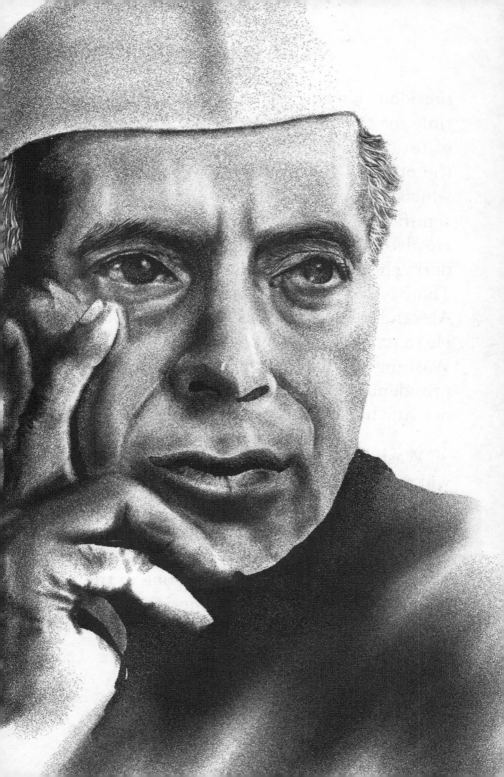

JAWAHARLAL NEHRU

BIRTH: *November 14, 1889*
Allahabad, India

DEATH: *May 27, 1964 (aged 74)*
Delhi, India

Jawaharlal Nehru was the first prime minister of independent India. He has been referred to as the 'Architect of Modern India'. He remains the longest serving prime minister of the country.

Jawaharlal Nehru was born on November 14, 1889, in Allahabad, India, to Motilal Nehru and Swarup Rani. Motilal Nehru himself was a part of the Indian independence movement. Jawaharlal's father served as the president of the Indian National Congress twice. Nehru received his early education at home till the age of fifteen, after which he went to Harrow School in England. For his higher education, Nehru attended Trinity College in Cambridge.

In 1910, Nehru went to London. There, he studied law at the Honourable Society of the Inner temple. In 1912, Nehru came back to India, having developed a sense of nationalism. He started his practice as a lawyer at the Allahabad High Court.

Nehru was not satisfied with how the Indian National Congress was functioning. Indian commoners were dominated by the English-knowing upper-class elite. Soon, he joined the civil rights movement launched by Gandhi, angered by the harsh treatment of his fellow Indians by the British. He suffered willingly for the sake of his country.

In 1917, Nehru joined the All India Home Rule League. He had immense support from Gandhi. He worked with the National Congress and was elected to the post of the general secretary of the Congress.

In 1920, the Non-Cooperation Movement was launched. It was started by Mahatma Gandhi and Nehru. For launching this movement, both of them were jailed for the first time. In 1929, Jawaharlal Nehru was named as the president of the Indian National Congress.

Nehru also took part in the Civil Disobedience movement. At the same time, Mahatma Gandhi started the *Satyagraha movement*, which was supported by Nehru. However he was once again imprisoned, along with a large number of nationalists. When World War II ended, Nehru asked for complete independence for India.

In 1947, India got independence and the British departed from Indian soil. But before they left, they divided the country into two nations, India and Pakistan.

Nehru became the first prime minister of the country soon after the country got independence. He made many changes in domestic, international, economic, agricultural and social policies. He built many renowned institutions and industries, which boosted the Indian economy and helped in its modernization. Nehru greatly emphasized on equality irrespective of caste, color or religion.

Nehru's main focus was education and the youth of the country. He felt that the youth were vital for the country's future growth. So he founded organizations of higher learning, such as the All India Institute of Medical Sciences (AIIMS), the Indian Institute of Technology (IIT), the Indian Institute of Management (IIM) and others. He introduced free and compulsory primary education to all children in his five-year plan.

Nehru also began the National Defence Academy and the Atomic Energy Commission of India (AEC). He strengthened the country with modern equipment and defense systems to safeguard the borders.

He also built good relations with the neighboring countries. Nehru supported the inclusion of the People's Republic of China as a permanent member in the Security Council of the United Nations. This helped in establishing friendly relations. But, it didn't last very long and soon border disputes arose. In 1962, China invaded India's northern border. It was known as the Sino-Indian War. The war and conflicts took a toll on Nehru's health.

In 1955, Nehru was awarded the Bharat Ratna Award, India's highest civilian honor. He received this award for his exceptional contribution to the freedom struggle.

Nehru married Kamala Kaul in 1916. They had one daughter, Indira Priyadarshini Nehru (later Gandhi), who became the first female prime minister of the country.

Nehru was very fond of children. He was addressed as 'Chacha Nehru' by children all over the country. In 1965, the Government of India introduced the Jawaharlal Nehru Award. Nehru died on May 27, 1964.

JOSIP BROZ TITO

BIRTH: May 7, 1892
Kumrovec, Croatia

DEATH: May 4, 1980
Ljubljana, Slovenia

Josip Broz Tito was the president of Yugoslavia and a communist revolutionary. Born on May 7, 1892 in Croatia to Franjo and Marija Broz, young Josip completed his primary education in 1905 and two years later, he shifted to Sisak to train as a locksmith's apprentice.

After completing his training, he joined the Social Democratic Party of Croatia and

Slavonia. However, in 1913, he was drafted into the Austro-Hungarian Army. After taking non-commissioned training, he was enrolled as a sergeant in the war against Serbia in 1914.

Within a year, Tito was promoted to sergeant major for his heroic acts. In 1915, he was sent to the Russian front, where he fought bravely before being caught by the Russian army. However, he was freed in 1917 when revolting workers broke into the prison.

On returning to Yugoslavia, he joined the Communist Party, which won the elections by 59 seats. However, the government banned communist activities and so, Tito had to move to Veliko Trojstvo.

In 1928, he was elected as the secretary of the Zagreb branch of the Metal Worker's Union of the CPY (Communist Party of Yugoslavia). Assuming the post, Tito carried out many anti-government activities in the form of street demonstrations and much more. As a result, he was arrested and sentenced to five years in prison. During his prison sentence, he met Moša

Pijade, who later became his role model. After leaving prison, he moved to Vienna and became a member of the CPY Politburo.

From 1935 to 1936, Tito worked under the orders of CPY Secretary General Milan Gorkic in the Soviet Union. During his rule, CPY gained attention and became increasingly powerful. However, Gorkic died in 1937 and Tito was appointed as CPY general secretary in 1939.

When the German invasion took place, it was only CPY that stood strong and asked the people to reunite and fight against it. Tito established a military committee within CPY; he was the commander-in-chief. Later, a treaty was signed, which led to the merger of CPY and King Peter's II government in exile. Soon after, Tito was appointed as the prime minister of Yugoslavia and the commander-in-chief of Yugoslavia's forces. In October 1944, the Soviet army, with the help of Tito, liberated Serbia, and by 1945, the Communist Party emerged as the only controller of Yugoslavia.

Tito believed that he could rule the country

by himself, without interference from the Soviet Union, but Stalin disagreed. Stalin strived to eliminate Tito from his role but to no avail. The rift between the two resulted in the country being cut off from the Soviet Union and other Eastern European nations. After the death of Stalin, Tito sought to strengthen ties with developing countries. He made Yugoslavia one of the founding members of the Non-Alignment Movement and formed strong ties with third world countries.

Tito officially changed the name of the country to the Socialist Federal Republic of Yugoslavia. He brought many changes to the country, giving people the right to speech and religious expression. In fact, in 1967, he abolished the need for a visa and opened the borders for foreign visitors. He also took an active part in promoting a peaceful resolution for the Israeli-Arab conflict.

In 1971, he was once again elected as the president. Under his rule, the constituent republics were responsible for healthcare, education, and housing, whereas the federal government was responsible for defense, foreign exchange, monetary affairs, and internal security. In 1974, he passed a new constitution which made him the president for life.

For his outstanding efforts, he received 98 international and 21 national decorations. He also received the French Legion of Honor and National Order of Merit, the Soviet Order of Lenin, the British Order of the Bath, the Japanese Order of the Chrysanthemum, the Order of Merit of Italy and the German Federal Cross of Merit.

Tito married thrice in his life and had four children. In 1979, he became increasingly ill. He breathed his last on May 4, 1980 and he was buried at the House of Flowers, in the museum of Yugoslav history in Belgrade, Serbia.

JOHN F. KENNEDY

BIRTH: *May 29, 1917*
Brookline, Massachusetts, USA

DEATH: *November 22, 1963 (aged 46)*
Dallas, Texas, USA

John F. Kennedy was the 35th President of the United States, best known for the Nuclear Test-Ban Treaty and the Alliance for Progress.

John Fitzgerald Kennedy was born on May 29, 1917 in Brookline, Massachusetts to Joseph P. Kennedy, Sr. and Rose Fitzgerald. He belonged to a wealthy and influential political family. His father was a banker and was later appointed as the first chairman of the US Securities and Exchange Commission (SEC). His mother was a socialite and philanthropist. As a child, he attended private schools such as the Canterbury School. In 1935, he enrolled at Princeton University but dropped out due to illness. The next year, he moved to Harvard.

During his time at Harvard, he took an interest in political philosophy. He wrote a thesis in 1940 called the *Appeasement at Munich*. It was well-received and soon turned into a book named *Why England Slept*. The book was a bestseller.

Kennedy joined the US Navy in 1941. In just a few years, he became a lieutenant. In 1943, Kennedy's boat was attacked by a Japanese warship. Kennedy showed great bravery when he rescued his crewmen and took them to a nearby island. For his courage, Kennedy was awarded the Navy and Marine Corps Medal and the Purple Heart Medal. After his complete recovery, Kennedy was released from duty.

Kennedy then began his political pursuits. In 1945, he started to work as a special correspondent for Hearst Newspapers. It proved to be fruitful and also brought him in the public domain. It was his father who supported him in his election to the US Congress in 1947. For the next six years, Kennedy worked as a congressman, and then became a US Senator in 1953.

Kennedy's time at the Senate was hard. He had major health issues, which troubled him most of his life. He took many leaves of absence from the Senate. During his leaves, Kennedy worked on his book titled *Profile in Courage*. The book became a bestseller and won him a Pulitzer Prize. Even though he loved to work as a senator, he was more interested in the larger picture. He desired to solve country-wide problems and international challenges.

In 1960, Kennedy fought for a presidency against the then Vice President Richard Nixon. He won the presidential elections by a narrow margin. It was the closest win in the history of elections. Kennedy became the 35th president of the United States, and the first president born in the twentieth century. The Kennedy presidency had a few significant events such as the building of the Berlin Wall in Germany, the Bay of Pigs invasion and the Cuban Missile Crisis.

During his presidency, he helped Cuban revolutionaries attack the communist Cuban leader Fidel Castro. The main motive of this program was to enable Cuban people to remove Castro from power. However, the plan failed as most of the attackers were either killed or captured. This event was named the Bay of Pigs invasion after the place where the invasion took place. Kennedy then formed a 'Special Group' and General Edward Lansdale was appointed as the advisory of the group. Lansdale's strategies were aimed at the removal of the Castro government.

Another major event in Kennedy's life as the president was the Cuban Missile Crisis. Around 1962, the United States discovered the Soviet Union's secret missile base in Cuba. It was a big threat for the US government, as the missiles could strike America anytime and it would have led to a nuclear war. Kennedy understood that if the US did not strike first, there would be a lot of damage due to the close range of the atomic weapons.

Kennedy solved the missile issue thoughtfully. To keep the missiles out of play, they made a compromise in which the Soviet Union agreed to dismantle their bases. The US also agreed never to invade Cuba and removed their missiles from Turkey.

In 1963, Kennedy introduced the Civil Rights bill. It was made for minorities and gave them access to public schools and protected their voting rights.

Kennedy married Jacqueline Bouvier in 1953. The couple had four children.

Kennedy was shot by Lee Harvey Oswald, and died on November 22, 1963 while he was on a political tour in Texas.

LEE KUAN YEW

BIRTH: *September 16, 1923*
Singapore

DEATH: *March 23, 2015 (aged 91)*
Singapore

Lee Kuan Yew was the founding father and the first prime minister of the Republic of Singapore. He adopted the policies of neutrality and non-violence while fighting for his country's independence.

Lee Kuan Yew was born to Lee Chin Koon and Chua Jim Neo on September 16, 1923. Kuan studied at the Raffles Institution, and gained the first position in the senior Cambridge exams in Singapore and Malaysia. He was awarded a scholarship to Raffles College, where he studied between 1940 to 1942. After the end of the Second World War, Kuan went to England and graduated with a 'double first' degree from the Fitzwilliam College.

Yew gained invaluable political experience while working in John Laycock's law firm upon his return to Singapore. And in 1954, he founded the People's Action Party (PAP) with educated middle-class men. He won the Tanjong Pagar seat and became the opposition leader in the elections held in 1955. In the 1959 national elections, the PAP won 43 out of 51 seats of the Legislative Assembly, making Yew the first prime minister of Singapore.

Yew established the Housing and Development Board (HDB) in 1960. The HDB took steps to provide affordable housing on war footing. He also supported the referendum to form a federation comprising of Singapore, Malaya, Sarawak and Sabah. The federation proposed by the Malaysian Prime Minister Tunku Abdul Rahman was formed in 1963, and it ended the

British colonial rule of Singapore. In 1965, however, due to a variety of reasons, including racial tension, Singapore was expelled from the federation. The Republic of Singapore was formed on August 9, 1965. Yew first solved the problem of limited natural resources in the Republic of Singapore. Two years later, he declared the policies of non-alignment and neutrality. He also ensured that the United Nations and Association of Southeast Asian Nations (ASEAN) accepted Singapore.

Yew introduced compulsory military service in 1967 by assigning the task of forming the Singapore Armed Forces to the Deputy Prime Minister, Goh Keng Swee. He encouraged the use of the English language in the country. To form the National University of Singapore, he united the English-language-based University of Singapore and the Chinese-language-based Nanyang University. In 1983, Yew established the Social Development Unit to provide opportunities to and encourage social interaction between educated men and women.

He resigned from the designation of prime minister in 1990 in favor of Goh Chok Tong, and became a senior minister in the cabinet. Later, Goh Chok Tong resigned and made way for Yew's oldest son, Lee Hsien Loong, and took the position of the 'minister mentor' in 2004.

Under the leadership of its first president, Singapore was industrialized with the help of foreign investment that provided cheap manpower, a modern transport system, highly skilled labor, and a communication network. The Economic Development Board was established in 1961. Singapore's per capita income and economy developed eightfold from 1965 to 1985. Homelessness, poverty-stricken families, and unemployment also reduced during these years.

Yew was honored with the Knight Grand Cross of the Order of St Michael and St George, Order of the Companions of Honor, and the Freedom of the City of London award by Britain. The Woodrow Wilson International Center for Scholars awarded him the Woodrow Wilson Award for his excellent public service.

Yew was fond of reading and loved Tom Clancy novels that were popular for military-science and espionage stories. During his lifetime, Yew penned many books. Some of these books are *From Third World to First, One Man's View of the World, The Singapore Story,* and *The Wit and Wisdom of Lee Kuan Yew.*

Lee Kuan Yew got married to Kwa Geok Choo in 1950. They were parents to three children who went on to become great personalities.

Lee Kuan Yew died on March 23, 2015 due to pneumonia, at the age of 91.

MARGARET THATCHER

BIRTH: *October 13, 1925*
Grantham, England

DEATH: *April 8, 2013 (aged 87)*
London, England

Margaret Thatcher was the first female prime minister of the United Kingdom. She was a leader of the Conservative Party. She was called the 'Iron Lady' because of her leadership style and radical beliefs.

Margaret Hilda Roberts was born on October 13, 1925, in Grantham, to Alfred Roberts and Beatrice Ethel. Her father was a grocer and the town mayor. She had one sibling. Margaret attended Kesteven Grantham Girls' School. She did exceptionally well academically and participated in many extra-curricular activities. In 1943, she went to Oxford College. There, Margaret was the president of the Oxford University Conservative Association and graduated with a degree in chemistry.

In 1950, Thatcher stood for Parliament elections for the first time. She was the youngest and the only female representative at the time. Margaret had major support from the public even though it was difficult to defeat the liberal Labor Party. She didn't win the first time, but tried as a Conservative candidate once more, only to be defeated again. In 1952, Thatcher studied law and qualified as a barrister, in 1953.

In 1959, she won her first election. Over the next few years, she rose in the ranks of the Conservative Party and joined the shadow cabinet in 1967. Thatcher was the secretary of state for education and helped in increasing the education budget and building more schools. In 1974, the Conservative Party lost power, which made Thatcher a dominant face in politics. She became the leader of the Conservative Party in 1975. She was finally elected as the prime minister on May 4, 1979.

The same year, Britain was going through an economic crisis. Thatcher adopted a new economic theory known as 'monetarism'. She also modified the government's control on businesses, taxation policies and money circulation. During the 1980s, the Thatcher government gained more favor after their success in the Falklands War. Argentina attacked Falkland Islands, a British Territory in 1982. Thatcher led Britain to victory, which raised her government's popularity. In 1983, after her re-election, she continued to employ her strict economic policies. Thatcher's government was known best for her set of policies and practices called 'Thatcherism'.

In 1984, a miners' strike took place. Thatcher had forced the workers to work with no allowances after their protest against 'uneconomic pits'. During this time, she also showed her dislike for the European Union's federalism. During her second term as prime minister, Thatcher worked through multiple crises. The most famous one being an assassination attempt against her.

She was elected for a third term in 1987. In her third term, she introduced new policies and changes in the tax system. But the new tax policies led to an economic imbalance within her party. Her power as prime minister declined in 1989. However, she continued implementing her ideas and refused to change the tax and labor laws.

The economic condition worsened and the cabinet wanted her to resign. She finally resigned in 1990. Next year, she was admitted to the House of Lords. She also wrote three books: *The Downing Street Years*, *The Path to Power*, and *Statecraft*. She explained her political experiences in these books.

Thatcher was made an honorary member of the Carlton Club. She was the first woman to get the full membership rights of the club. She received the highest civilian honor, the

Presidential Medal of Freedom from the United States in 1991. In 1992, *Time* magazine included her in the list of '100 most important people of the 20th century'. In 1998, she received the Ronald Reagan Freedom Award.

She married Sir Denis Thatcher in 1951. They had twins. After the death of her husband, Margaret became a hermit and avoided public appearances. She died on April 8, 2013 at the age of 87, in London, after she suffered a stroke.

MARTIN LUTHER KING, JR.

BIRTH: *January 15, 1929*
Atlanta, Georgia, USA

DEATH: *April 4, 1968 (aged 39)*
Memphis, Tennessee, USA

Martin Luther King, Jr. was a social activist and Baptist minister. He was a leader of the African-American civil rights movement in the 1950s and 60s.

Martin Luther King, Jr. was born on January 15, 1929, in Atlanta, Georgia to Martin Luther

King, Sr. and Alberta Williams King. His father was a pastor in a church and a civil rights leader. His mother was a former school teacher. For his education, he went to Booker T. Washington High School. He was such an excellent student that he skipped two grades in high school. At the age of fifteen, he went to Morehouse College. Martin graduated with a degree in sociology. He continued his education and attended the Crozer Seminary, and later Boston University. In 1955, he received his PhD.

In 1954, Martin Luther joined the Dexter Avenue Baptist Church and became a pastor. He was also selected as an official member of the National Association for the Advancement of Colored People (NAACP). The first major civil rights protest campaign was the Montgomery bus boycott. It started after a black lady named Rosa Parks declined to give up her seat in a bus to a white man. There was major discrimination in all public spaces at the time; even the bus seats were segregated so as to ensure that whites do not mingle with African-Americans. Parks was arrested for her bold move.

The boycott placed an economic strain on the public transit system. King became the protest's leader and official spokesman. It went on for over a year. In the process, King was imprisoned, even his house was bombed. King handled the situation and the protest came to an end.

After the boycott was successful, King and other civil rights activists founded an organization in 1957, called the Southern Christian Leadership Conference (SCLC). The group was formed to organize African-American churches to conduct non-violent protests.

King was also a great orator. He delivered many speeches on racism and other sensitive issues. He met different religious and fellow civil rights leaders through his outreach. During 1959, he met the family members and followers of Gandhi. King described this encounter in his autobiography. He wrote many books and articles during this time. King's first book was *Stride Toward Freedom: The Montgomery Story* (1958).

He continued to work tirelessly with his SCLC partners. He also took part in one of the most important civil rights battles of the 1960s. He was part of the non-violence movement, especially during the Birmingham campaign of 1963. He came up with a civil rights declaration called the 'Letter from Birmingham Jail'.

In 1963, King organized the famous 'March on Washington', in which thousands of people marched to show their support for the civil rights movement. King raised issues like discrimination in public schools, protection from police harassment and prejudice in employment. He gave his legendary speech containing the much-quoted words "I have a dream". It is one of the most influential speeches in history. The March on Washington was also successful. His last address was called "I've been to the Mountaintop".

He visited Jamaica in 1965, and then spent some more time there in 1967 to write his last book, *Where Do We Go from Here: Chaos or Community?* King was named the 'Person of the Year' by *Time* magazine in 1963. In 1964, he became the youngest person to be awarded the Nobel Peace Prize. In 1977, King received the Presidential Medal of Freedom. The Congressional Gold Medal was awarded to him posthumously in 2004.

King married Coretta Scott in 1953. She was a singer, author and a civil rights activist herself. The couple had four children.

King died on April 4, 1968 at the age of 39 in Memphis, Tennessee. He was shot while he was standing in a motel's second-floor balcony. After his death, many of his followers participated in a nationwide riot. His wife took up the leadership of the civil rights movement. Coretta Scott became an active member of the women's movement and the LGBT rights movement.

To pay tribute to this great leader, the National Civil Rights Museum was built. Several streets were also named after him. The third Monday of January was declared as a national holiday to honor Martin Luther King, Jr.

MAXIMILIEN ROBESPIERRE

BIRTH: *May 6, 1758*
Arras, France

DEATH: *July 28, 1794*
Paris, France

Maximilien Robespierre was a major political figure in eighteenth century France. He was a French lawyer who became one of the most influential figures in the French Revolution. Robespierre served as a member of the Committee of Public Safety. He grew up with strong moral values, which further helped him to fight against the death penalty and advocate the abolishment of slavery. Being a revolutionary at heart, Robespierre joined politics and fought against monarchy, following which monarchy was abolished and France was finally declared a republic.

Maximilien Robespierre was born on May 6, 1758 to François Maximilien Barthélémy de Robespierre and Jacqueline Marguerite Carrault. His father was a lawyer at the Conseil d'Artois. Maximilien was the eldest child out of four siblings.

Robespierre lost his mother at a young age, following which his father abandoned them. They grew up at their paternal aunt's home. At the age of eight, Robespierre went to middle school at Arras for his primary education. Later he was recommended by the Bishop for a scholarship to the Lycée Louis-le-Grand in Paris in 1769. He was trained in law and politics at the university. He graduated at the age of 23.

As a student, the philosopher Jean-Jacques Rousseau inspired Robespierre. Fascinated by his thoughts and writing, Robespierre adopted many of his philosophies and values.

Robespierre was admitted to the Arras bar

after the completion of his legal studies. He was appointed as a judge in the criminal court of the Diocese of Arras in March 1782. However, he was opposed to death penalty, which caused him to eventually resign.

With time, he became an amazing advocate. He further fought for the rights of men and campaigned for the ideals of enlightenment of the public. Following this, he ventured into politics and was elected as a deputy of the Third Estate. Robespierre soon became popular for his attacks on the French monarchy and his democratic reforms.

In April 1789, Robespierre became the president of the powerful Jacobin political faction. The following years, Robespierre spent his time writing the *Declaration of Rights of Man and Citizen*, which later became a part of the French Constitution.

During the rule of King Louis XVI, Robespierre actively protested against the monarchy and freed people from the king's rule. Later, he was announced as the head of the Paris delegation for the National Convention. On September 21, 1792, France was declared a republic. Following this, the king was put on trial for treason and finally executed in January 1793.

After the king's execution, Robespierre's influence increased manifold. Soon, the need for a state government increased. The Jacobins established a Revolutionary Tribunal in March 1793. They replaced the Committee of General Defense with the Committee of Public Safety, of which Robespierre became a member.

Soon, Robespierre became an important member of the committee. A period known as the 'Reign of Terror' then started around September 1793. The Reign of Terror was an attempt to remove all those who opposed the revolution. Massacres and many public executions took place, and after 1793, Robespierre became one of the most hated figures in the country.

Followed by the unprecedented violence unleashed on the country under the Reign of Terror, the Thermidorian Reaction, a counterrevolution, commenced in 1794. It was a coup d'état against the dominating members of the Jacobin club who were central to the Committee of Public Safety. Robespierre was accused of being the planner of the Reign of Terror. He was arrested along with others who were accused of the same, like Louis Antoine de Saint-Just.

Later, Robespierre was declared an outlaw, executed and condemned without judicial process. He was executed on July 28, 1794. Robespierre's life ended in one of the most radical phases of the French Revolution.

MIKHAIL GORBACHEV

BIRTH: March 2, 1931
Privolnoye, Russia

Mikhail Gorbachev is a former Soviet politician and the last leader of the Soviet Union. He played a key role in the fall of the Berlin Wall and in re-unifying East and West Germany. He is also a Nobel Peace Prize winner and the co-founder of the Gorbachev Foundation, and Green Cross International.

Mikhail Gorbachev was born on March 2, 1931 in Russia. His father, Sergey Andreyevich Gorbachev, was a World War II veteran and his mother, Maria Panteleyevna Gorbacheva, was a *kolkhoz* (a collective farm) worker. From a young age, Gorbachev was interested in operating machines. In 1948, he contributed to the house income heftily by harvesting a record crop, making Gorbachev the youngest person to win the Order of the Red Banner of Labor.

After completing high school with a silver medal, Gorbachev enrolled at Moscow State University in 1950. He earned his degree in law in 1955. He pursued a correspondence course and received a master's diploma from Stavropol Institute of Agriculture in 1967. Soon, he became a trained agricultural economist.

He became a Communist Party member when he was studying in high school and was granted complete membership in 1952. He slowly rose up the ranks within the Communist Party in the 1950s and 60s, and in 1970, Gorbachev became the party secretary of the Stravopol Kraikom. He improved the living standards of the working class and helped them expand private plots and organize collective farms. In 1985, the Politburo elected him as the general secretary after the death of Andropov and his successor Konstantin Chernenko. As the secretary, Gorbachev reformed the party by introducing restructuring, democratization and openness. Not only this, but Gorbachev also brought about many technological developments for reducing waste and enhancing productivity. He led an anti-alcohol campaign and established a socially-oriented market economy.

Gorbachev, on his part, helped end the Cold War by reaching a compromise with Ronald Reagan, who was the president of the United States. Gorbachev signed a treaty with Reagan in 1987, intending to bring peace between the two countries by destroying their respective stocks of nuclear-tipped missiles.

He was also behind the formation of the Congress of People's Deputies, a new bicameral parliament, to restructure the government. His reformative policies gained him a real standing with the Supreme Soviet hence elected, which made him its chairman, in 1989. And in 1990, he was elected as the president by the Congress of People's Deputies.

As the president of the Soviet Union, Gorbachev mainly focused on making peaceful international relations. He contributed to the reunification of Germany and the end of the Cold War. He also advanced economic reforms and various domestic matters. While he was dealing with issues within his country, the opposition leader Boris Yeltsin became strong competition for him. Yeltsin wanted to bring a radical change in the economy. Soon, Yeltsin gained the position of the president of the Russian Federation by vote. In a series of events, Yeltsin gained the support of the committee and the people, which led to Gorbachev stepping down as president. Soon after he handed over the position to Yeltsin, the Soviet Union dissolved.

After the end of his presidency, Gorbachev formed the Social Democratic Party of Russia. He resigned from the party in 2004 and went on to form another political party named the Union of Social Democrats.

Gorbachev was awarded the Nobel Peace

Prize on October 15, 1990 for his 'excellent leadership skills and outstanding contributions to the advancement of the world'. He received the Order of St Andrew, Russia's highest state decoration, in 2011. He also received a number of other honors and awards, including three Orders of Lenin, the Indira Gandhi Prize for Peace, Disarmament and Development and the Ronald Reagan Freedom Award.

Mikhail Gorbachev is married to a college friend from Moscow State University, Raisa Titarenko. They tied the knot in 1953. Four years later, they were blessed with a daughter.

MAHATMA GANDHI

BIRTH: October 2, 1869
Porbandar, India

DEATH: January 30, 1948 (aged 78)
Delhi, India

Mohandas Karamchand Gandhi was an Indian lawyer who became the primary leader of India's independence movement. Gandhi not only led India to independence from British rule, but also inspired movements for civil rights and freedom all across the world.

Mohandas Karamchand Gandhi was born on October 2, 1869 in Porbandar, India, to Karamchand Uttamchand Gandhi and Putlibai.

His father was the Diwan (a treasury officer) of Porbandar. His mother was a religious lady who had a significant influence on Gandhi. He was an average student in school. But he still won prizes and scholarships. In 1887, Gandhi attended Samaldas College.

The following year, he went to study law at the Inner Temple in London. After Gandhi completed his degree, he came back to India in 1891. He took up a job in an Indian law firm called Dada Abdulla & Co. For his job, he had to shift to South Africa, which was a part of the British Empire in 1893. The time Gandhi spent in South Africa helped him begin his work in civil rights.

He had very revealing spiritual and political experiences in South Africa, which shaped the latter part of his life. Gandhi realized that people of color were subjected to immense discrimination. He witnessed such prejudice once when he was asked to move from the first-class compartment of a train only because of his skin color, even though he had a valid ticket. Events like these inspired him to fight for social justice.

In 1915, he came back to India. In the next few years, he joined the Indian National Congress and became one of the most powerful figures in the Indian political scene. He was against violence and believed that civil disobedience could stop the British rule. Many of these campaigns were directed by Gandhi. Thus, a large portion of the Indian population refused to work, sat on the streets and went on strikes. It had an enormous impact on the British Empire. Gandhi united all of the Indian, irrespective of religion, caste and beliefs, in the country's fight for independence. He promoted non-cooperation with British rule and avoided all British goods in favor of Indian-made products. He also boycotted British educational systems and advised Indians to resign from government jobs.

In 1930, Gandhi started a new civil disobedience campaign against the colonial government. The British government had introduced the 'salt tax', which prohibited Indians from collecting and selling salt from their own lands. This significantly affected India's poorest citizens. Gandhi started a march from Ahmedabad to Dandi in Gujarat in protest of this law. Thousands of Indians joined him on this march. Next was the Quit India Movement during World War II in 1942. He demanded British withdrawal from India. The Quit India Movement is seen as the most powerful movement in the history of the Indian independence struggle.

Gandhi fought till the Britishers quit India. But, the Muslim League demanded an independent Islamic state. Gandhi opposed the idea of separation. He was very bothered by the thought of partition and tried his best to unite Indians of different religions and communities. In 1946, the Muslim League called for a Direct Action Day. It caused a riot between the Hindus and Muslims in Calcutta. Gandhi personally tried to stop the riot. The Direct Action Day was the worst public riot that British India had ever seen.

On August 15, 1947, India got independence. However, it was divided into two nations: India and Pakistan.

Gandhi was a great writer and wrote many books such as, *The Story of My Experiments with Truth, Satyagraha in South Africa* and *Hind Swaraj or Indian Home Rule*. In Gandhi's honor, Rabindranath Tagore, a great Indian polymath, gave him the title 'Mahatma' which means 'great soul'. Gandhi was often called the 'Father of the Nation' in India and also fondly referred to as 'Bapu'.

Gandhi married Kasturba Makhanji Kapadia in 1883 when he was only thirteen years old. The couple had five children, but one died in infancy. Gandhi's wife also became a social activist later in life.

Gandhi was assassinated on January 30, 1948 by the militant Hindu nationalist Nathuram Godse at Birla House in New Delhi.

MUHAMMAD ALI JINNAH

BIRTH: December 25, 1876
Karachi, Pakistan

DEATH: September 11, 1948 (aged 71)
Karachi, Pakistan

Muhammad Ali Jinnah was an Indian-Pakistani politician. Jinnah was the founder and the first governor-general of Pakistan. He was known as the 'great leader'.

Muhammad Ali Jinnah was born on December 25, 1876 in Karachi, Pakistan to Poonja bhai and Mithibai. He started his formal education at the age of six. He attended the Sind Madrassat al Islam. He changed many schools before he moved to the Christian Missionary Society High School at the age of sixteen. Jinnah continued his studies and went to the University of Bombay.

In 1892, Jinnah was offered work as an apprentice in Sir Frederick Leigh Croft's Graham's Shipping and Trading Company. He moved to London for the job. After Jinnah worked there for a short while, he decided to leave the job. He wanted to become a lawyer. He entered Lincoln's Inn, one of the best legal organizations that prepared students for the bar examination. However, his time in London was unpleasant. Jinnah experienced two big losses, the deaths of his wife and his mother.

Still, he completed his studies and frequently visited the House of Commons. Jinnah started to take an interest in political matters. He was influenced by William E. Gladstone, who was the prime minister at that time. At the age of twenty, his law career started to thrive. He received an invitation from the advocate-general of Bombay.

In 1900, he got a chance to work with the

Bombay Presidency magistrate for a short while. During his time there, he established himself as a lawyer.

Jinnah began to take part in political affairs after he attended the 20th Indian National Congress annual meeting in 1904. For the next two years, he served as a member of the Congress and took part in the Indian independence movement. Around 1909, he was admitted to the Imperial Legislative Council as Bombay's Muslim member. It was a stepping stone towards a long and great parliamentary career for Jinnah.

He also met the great Congress leader Gopal Krishna Gokhale, a famous Maratha leader. Gokhale had greatly influenced Jinnah. In 1913, he was sent to England on account of the Congress, which was directed by Gokhale. He was welcomed as an ambassador of Hindu-Muslim unity by Congress leaders.

In 1916, he became the president of the Muslim League. He signed the Lucknow Pact on behalf of the League. The major focus of Jinnah's political career was to raise India's status in the international community. He wanted to develop a sense of Indian nationhood amongst the people of India. In 1923, he became the Muslim spokesperson from Bombay in the Central Legislative Assembly. His time in the parliament was very effective and he started to work with the Swaraj Party.

By 1926, a few issues started to arise between the Congress and Jinnah since he supported the idea of separate electorates for Muslims. In 1930, the Muslim-majority states in the Indian subcontinent began to demand statehood. This demand was started by Sir Muhammad Iqbal. In the next ten years, Jinnah proposed the separation of states at the Muslim League Conference. He asked for a single separate Muslim state with a majority of the Muslim population. In 1942, the Muslim League sided with Jinnah in this quest.

The British government wanted to maintain the political unity of the Indian subcontinent, but that didn't happen. Ultimately both the Congress and the British government agreed to the partition of India. On August 14, 1947, Pakistan took birth as an independent nation.

Jinnah became the governor-general of the newly formed Muslim state. He emerged as a great authoritative figure who built a young nation from its very foundation. He was honored as the 'Father of the Nation'. But he couldn't continue his efforts towards making a stronger Pakistan. In the formative years of Pakistan, his health started to decline.

In 1925, he was knighted by Lord Reading, an honor which he eventually rejected. His famed quote was, "I prefer to be plain Mr. Jinnah."

Jinnah married twice and had a daughter. He died on September 11, 1948 in Karachi, after suffering from tuberculosis.

MUSTAFA KEMAL ATATÜRK

BIRTH: 1881
Salonika, Greece

DEATH: November 10, 1938
Istanbul, Turkey

Mustafa Kemal Atatürk was the first president of Turkey, a revolutionary statesman, and an author who helped in establishing the Republic of Turkey. He led the war of independence in Turkey and modernized the country with his policies and reforms, which came to be known as "Kemalism".

Mustafa Kemal Atatürk was born in 1881 as Ali Rıza oğlu Mustafa to Ali Riza and Zubeyde Hanim. He grew up in Salonika, in the Ottoman Empire. At twelve, Mustafa was sent to a military academy in Istanbul. His mathematics teacher gave him his second name 'Kemal', which means 'perfection'.

He graduated in 1905. Shortly after, he was arrested for his anti-monarchist activities. After his release, he joined a secret revolutionary society called Vatan ve Hürriyet meaning 'Motherland and Liberty'. In July 1908, he participated in the Young Turks Revolution, which deposed Sultan Abdul Hamid II and established a constitutional monarchy. Atatürk held various posts in the Ottoman army from 1909 to 1918. In 1911, he fought in the Italo-Turkish war. He also fought in the Balkan wars from 1912 to 1913. He was given the position of the commander of the 19th division in the First World War. Atatürk's military prowess and bravery helped him in thwarting Allied invasions of the Dardanelles and earned him repeated promotions until the end of the fight in 1918.

After the end of the First World War, Atatürk planned and led a resistance movement to attain complete independence of Turkey. In a series of battles against the Armenian and Greek forces, Atatürk showed his strategic prowess and signed the Treaty of Lausanne. After that, he established the Republic of Turkey.

In 1923, Atatürk became the president of Turkey. He instituted social, political and economic reforms after establishing the Republic. Under his presidency, the Muslim state was transformed into a secular and democratic nation-state. He also formed a constitution that separated religion from the government and declared state secularism.

Atatürk insisted on the usage of Latin instead of Arabic and the use of Turkish for prayers. He also replaced the Islamic calendar with the Gregorian calendar. Besides this, he insisted that people accept westernization and abandon the Middle Eastern sartorial tradition. Under his rule, women were given equal political and civil rights. He gave orders to the

Ministry of National Education to ban religious schools and establish secular schools instead.

Atatürk was the visionary behind the establishment of the Central Bank of the Republic of Turkey. The first and second five-year economic plan was also supervised by him. Atatürk was known for solving all foreign issues without the use of military might. He promoted national sovereignty and the reformation of the political system by abolishing the Caliphate. His motto was, "Peace at home, Peace in the world."

For all his memorable work, Atatürk received many high profile decorations from the Turkish government, like the Silver Imtiyaz Medal, Golden Liakat Medal, Fifth Class Knight Order of the Medjidie, Medal of Independence, Gallipoli Star, and others. France bestowed upon him the Legion of Honor; and Bulgaria, the Commander Grand Cross Order of Saint Alexander. He also received the 1st and 2nd Class Iron Cross of the German Empire.

It is believed that Atatürk was in a relationship with Eleni Karinte and Fikriye Hanim, before he got married to Latife Usakligil in 1923. Their union was not a happy one, which is why they separated in 1925. Since he had no biological children, Atatürk adopted thirteen children; one son and twelve daughters. His daughter, Sabiha Gökçen, became one of Turkey's first female pilots and the world's first female fighter pilot.

From 1937 to 1938, Ataturk's health deteriorated drastically. Later, he was diagnosed with cirrhosis of the liver. He breathed his last at the age of 57 on November 10, 1938.

UNESCO honored Atatürk by naming his centennial birth year as the Atatürk Year. The government of Turkey has constructed many memorials, monuments, and squares in his honor. In Turkey, people fondly remember the first president as the 'Father of the Turks'.

NELSON MANDELA

BIRTH: *July 18, 1918*
Mvezo, South Africa

DEATH: *December 5, 2013 (aged 95)*
Johannesburg, South Africa

Nelson Mandela was an activist and the former president of South Africa who became a global advocate for human rights. He was deeply involved in anti-colonial politics and anti-apartheid movements.

Nelson Rolihlahla Mandela, also known as Nelson Mandela, was born on July 18, 1918, to Nosekeni Fanny and Gadla Henry

Mphakanyiswa. At the age of seven, Mandela was sent to a Methodist school where he got his first name 'Nelson' from a teacher. Post his father's death, his mother entrusted him to Chief Jongintaba Dalindyebo who treated Mandela as his own child.

After completing his secondary education, he attended the University of Fort Hare but did not receive a degree then because of his boycott against university policies and involvement in the Student Representative Council. He did receive it later. In 1941, Mandela moved to Johannesburg where he worked for Walter Sisulu, an African National Congress activist.

After completing his graduation via correspondence in 1943, Mandela enrolled in the University of Witwatersrand to pursue his legal studies. He also joined ANC under the influence of Sisulu. It was during this time that Nelson got actively involved in the anti-apartheid movement. He suggested the formation of a youth wing in ANC, which led to the foundation of the African National Congress Youth League (ANCYL). The organization was established with the motive to use new and better methods like strikes, boycotts, non-cooperation, and civil disobedience. In 1950, Mandela was appointed as the president of ANCYL.

Highly influenced by Mahatma Gandhi's non-violence movement, Mandela fought against apartheid by formulating the Defiance Campaign with many Communist groups. The government counterattacked Mandela's campaign by permitting mass arrest and martial law. The government also banned J. B. Marks, the ANU president, from making any public appearances, after which Mandela took the position of the president as his successor.

Mandela was imprisoned several times for his active involvement in the anti-apartheid movement. He was also given a suspended prison sentence for his 'Defiance Campaign against Unjust Laws' in 1952. Mandela was banned from attending any meetings or talking to a group of people for six months. During this time, Mandela received his law degree and started working with a firm called Terblanche and Briggish. Later, he established a law firm with Oliver Tambo named

Mandela and Tambo. The firm commonly dealt with police brutality cases.

In 1955, Mandela formed the Congress of the People and soon, in 1956, he and other ANC activists were sentenced for getting involved in treasonous acts against the state. Six years later, the trial proved them not guilty.

From 1961 to 1962, Mandela disguised himself and traveled through the country to spread awareness about the mass stay-at-home strike. He also formed the new cell structure for ANC known as 'Umkhonto we Sizwe (Spear of the Nation)' or MK. In February 1962, Mandela was chosen as the delegate of ANC for the Pan-African Freedom Movement for East, South and Central Africa. After returning from the tour, Mandela was imprisoned for illegally exiting from the country and was sent to Robben Island Prison near Cape Town.

On February 11, 1990, Mandela was released from prison by President F. W. de Klerk. Soon after his release, Mandela resumed office at ANC and was elected as the president of ANC.

In 1994, when South Africa held its democratic elections for the first time, Nelson Mandela won and became the first black president of the country. As a president, he worked diligently towards terminating apartheid and establishing a new constitution. He expanded healthcare services, combated poverty, and encouraged land reforms. On the international front, Mandela became a bridge between the United Kingdom and Libya.

Mandela did not contest for a second term, and instead served at healthcare centers and schools for public benefit. Later, he founded the Mandela Foundation and also helped victims in the Burundi civil war.

Mandela married thrice in his lifetime. His first wife, Evelyn Ntoko Mase, divorced him in 1958. In 1958, he got married to Winnie Madikizela-Mandela. They divorced in 1996. Mandela got married to Graca Machel on his eightieth birthday. He died on December 5, 2013 due to a respiratory illness.

SIMÓN BOLÍVAR

BIRTH: *July 24, 1783*
Caracas, Venezuela

DEATH: *December 17, 1830 (aged 47)*
Santa Marta, Colombia

Simón Bolívar was a famous Venezuelan soldier and statesman. He was the president of the Gran Colombia and the dictator of Peru. He is known for his liberation movement in six nations against the Spanish Empire.

Simón Bolívar was born on July 24, 1783 in Caracas, Venezuela. He belonged to a wealthy family. His family worked in sugar plantations and owned silver, gold and copper mines. Simon lost his father at a very young age. He was placed under the custody of a teacher for a short while. He received private lessons from some of the most famous teachers, one of them being Don Simon Rodriguez. Don influenced Simon's life as a friend and a mentor. Simon learned how to swim and ride horses from his teacher. He developed an interest in human rights, politics, history and sociology.

At the age of fourteen, Simon entered the military academy Milicias de Veraguas. In 1800, he moved to Madrid for his studies and remained there for the next two years. He learned the military tactics that helped him later in his battles. Around 1804, he went to France. When he was in Paris, Bolívar saw the coronation of Napoleon Bonaparte at Notre Dame. The event left a deep impression on him. He thought about the liberation of the people of his native place.

In 1807, Bolívar returned to Venezuela, which had just obtained de facto independence. There, he began his political career.

Bolívar was given the rank of colonel. Many

Spanish pioneers saw this as an opportunity to cut their ties with Spain. Bolívar also participated in many conspiratorial meetings. In 1810, the Spanish governor was officially expelled from Venezuela. A junta took over and the government needed help, so they sent Bolívar on a mission to London. Bolívar was asked to obtain arms and support from England. His visit to England was a fruitful one.

In 1811, he welcomed Francisco de Miranda, who was a major part of the war, as the general of the revolutionary army. During the war, Bolívar lost control of San Felipe Fort. He left his post and fled to his estate in San Mateo.

Miranda signed a deal with the enemy and surrendered to them. Bolívar and the other officers termed Miranda's actions as treasonous. They handed Miranda over to the Spanish Royal Army. Somehow, Bolívar also got a passport to flee the country and went to New Granada (present-day Colombia). There, he published his first written work called *The Cartagena Manifesto*. The book was based on the fall of Venezuela's First Republic.

Bolívar soon received the support of the nationalists of New Granada and decided to regain control of Venezuela. The Admirable Campaign was started on June 24, 1813 to form the Venezuelan Second Republic. Bolívar successfully defeated the Royalists in six battles.

The fight for independence soon began. A fierce civil war broke out. In 1814, a revolution headed by Jose Tomas Boves, a Spanish commander, led to the fall of the Venezuelan Republic. Bolívar had to return to New Granada. However, Bolívar fled to Haiti the very next year. There, he met Alexandre Petion, who agreed to help him in the war. In 1816, Alexandre helped Bolívar to return to Venezuela.

In 1819, Bolívar attended a meeting with the Congress that had assembled in Angostura. He went on to fight two battles and won both of them. They were the Battle of Carabobo in 1821 and the Battle of Pinchincha in 1822. After the war ended, Bolívar asked the lawmakers to declare the creation of a new state. After he defeated the Spanish army, the Republic of Colombia was established in just three days. It included the three departments of New Granada, Venezuela and Quito (Ecuador).

In 1824, Bolívar became the dictator of Peru. The next year, the country of Bolivia was founded. Bolívar is one of the few leaders who has a country named after him. He was a great leader, but faced many difficulties while dealing with Gran Colombia.

Bolívar married Maria Teresa Rodriguez in 1802. However, she passed away a few months into their marriage. Bolívar died on December 17, 1830 due to tuberculosis.

THOMAS JEFFERSON

BIRTH: *April 13, 1743*
Shadwell, Virginia, USA

DEATH: *July 4, 1826 (aged 83)*
Monticello, Virginia, USA

Thomas Jefferson was a Founding Father of the United States. He was one of the creators of the Declaration of Independence.

Thomas Jefferson was born on April 13, 1743 in Shadwell, Virginia to Peter Jefferson and Jane Randolph Jefferson. From a very young age, he was an avid reader and loved to explore nature. He also learned to play the violin and knew different languages such as Greek, French and

Latin. When Jefferson was eleven years, old he lost his father. He inherited his father's assets, including a huge piece of land, and started managing them.

Thomas got his formal education in science and history. Later he went to the College of William and Mary in Virginia. He studied law under a respected Virginia lawyer. After he completed his law degree in 1767, Jefferson started working as a lawyer. By 1773, he had handled many cases and was counted amongst the reputed lawyers of Virginia.

The early 1770s, were the beginning of his political career. The American colonies were being wrongly treated by the British rulers. Jefferson became a leader and decided to fight for their independence. In 1775, he became a delegate at the Second Continental Congress. The same year, the American Revolution of independence started. Jefferson wrote the first draft of the Declaration of Independence and the other members of the committee made some changes and presented it to the Congress. It is the most prized document in the history of the United States.

In 1779, Jefferson became the governor of Virginia. A significant change at the time was that the capital of the state changed from Williamsburg to Richmond. The same year, he was appointed as the first professor of law at the College of William and Mary. In 1785, Jefferson worked as a minister to France. As a minister, Jefferson helped France and Britain during the war. In 1790, Jefferson became the first secretary of state, when George Washington was president. He supported the state and local governments. He co-founded the Democratic-Republican Party to fight Hamilton's Federalist Party.

In 1796, Jefferson competed against John Adams in the presidential elections. He received the second highest votes, which made him vice-president. During this period the federalists wanted a war with France. The new Alien and Sedition Acts were passed in 1798, in which taxes were introduced. Jefferson criticized this act and attacked federalists. He believed that federalists had no right to use such power to exploit the public.

In 1801, Jefferson became the third president of the United States. The first thing he did right after he became president, was to reduce the federal budget. He wanted to give the power back to the states. He also reduced taxes, for which he became favorable amongst people. One of his main achievements, as president, was the Louisiana Purchase. Jefferson purchased a huge piece of land (Louisiana), from Napoleon Bonaparte of France. This purchase expanded the area under United States.

The second monumental event was the Lewis and Clark Expedition from 1804-06. Jefferson wished to map the area of the land he had acquired, and nominated captain Meriwether Lewis and second lieutenant William Clark to explore the western territory with a selected group of army volunteers.

Another major event was battling pirates from 1801-05, during the First Barbary War between the United States and Libya. During his presidency, he sent American navy ships off the coast of North Africa to battle pirate ships. These Barbary pirate ships had been attacking American merchant vessels for quite some time. Jefferson decided to put a stop to it and thus began the First Barbary War.

In 1801, he published *A Manual of Parliamentary Practice*, and its second edition in 1812. Unfortunately, the Library of Congress was burnt down by the British. So, Jefferson's vast collection of books was converted into a new library. The library was named after him.

Jefferson died on July 4, 1826 at the age of 83 in Virginia. He died on the same day as his fellow Founding Father, John Adams. It was also the 50th anniversary of the Declaration of Independence.

WINSTON CHURCHILL

BIRTH: *November 30, 1874*
Blenheim Palace, Oxfordshire, England

DEATH: *January 24, 1965 (aged 90)*
London, England

Winston Churchill was a British statesman, leader and author. He is recognized as one of the greatest political leaders of the twentieth century. His excellent leadership helped the country stand firm against Hitler and the Germans.

Sir Winston Leonard Spencer Churchill was born on November 30, 1874 in Oxfordshire, England to Lord Randolph and Jennie Jerome.

He belonged to a family of wealthy aristocrats and came from a long line of English politicians. His father was a politician in the British government. Lord Randolph held many high positions and was a famous figure in Tory politics.

Winston attended the Harrow Prep School as a child. In school he developed an interest in the English language. Later, he went to Royal Military College, Sandhurst and graduated in 1894. After graduation, he joined the British Army. Being in the army, Winston traveled all around the British Empire. He traveled to many places as a soldier. He went on to work as a war-time newspaper correspondent. He wrote stories about battles and his experiences in the military.

In 1896, Churchill moved to British India. He worked as both a soldier and a journalist. He established himself as a successful writer. In 1898, Churchill published his first book, *The Story of the Malakand Field Force*. It was about his experiences in India's North-west Frontier Province. *The Morning Post* wanted Churchill to cover the Boer War in South Africa. However, he was captured by enemy soldiers and became a prisoner of war. He somehow escaped prison and was rescued. After this incident, he rose to fame for a while and became a hero in Britain. He wrote about his experiences in the book *London to Ladysmith via Pretoria* (1900). By the time he returned to England, he had already published five books.

Churchill proved to be a great writer. But after publishing five books, he fully focused on his political career. In 1900, Churchill was nominated for the Parliament and joined the House of Commons as a Conservative. But four years later, he moved to the Liberal Party. During World War II, Churchill became the first lord in command of the Royal Navy. The prime minister of the time wanted to pacify Germany and Hitler. But, Churchill warned the government about their chances of failure and advised that they needed to fight Hitler, lest Hitler take over all of Europe someday.

In 1940, Germany invaded and took over control of Norway. During this time, Arthur

Neville Chamberlain was the prime minister. After the invasion, Chamberlain resigned and Churchill became the prime minister in 1940. He very smartly handled the situation of the German invasion and refused to sign a peace treaty with the Nazis. He also played a significant role in motivating the British Empire. He was a great orator. In one of his speeches, he warned people that the Battle of Britain was about to begin. With Churchill's leadership, the British held off Hitler and eventually defeated the Germans.

After the war, Churchill was no longer the prime minister. But he continued to work in the government. In 1951, he again became the prime minister. In 1954, he introduced new reforms such as the Mines and Quarries Act of 1954 and the Housing Repairs and Rent Act of 1955.

Churchill's major literary works include his series titled *The Second World War* (1948–53). The series was a great success and even won the Nobel Prize for Literature in 1953. It made Churchill famous as a writer in both Britain and the United States. In 1963, he became an honorary citizen of the United States.

Churchill married Clementine Hozier in 1908. They were happily married and had four children.

A few years later, Churchill's health began to deteriorate. He died on January 24, 1965 after he suffered from a stroke. Churchill's funeral was the largest state funeral in world history at the time. Churchill, around the time of his death, was worried about the Soviet Union and the Red Army. He predicted that as soon as World War II ended, a Cold War between the Western Nations of NATO (such as Britain, France, USA) and the communist Soviet Union would commence. This prediction proved to be true.

YASSER ARAFAT

BIRTH: August 24, 1929,
Cairo, Egypt

DEATH: November 11, 2004 (aged 75)
Paris, France

Yasser Arafat was a leader, a revolutionist and a diplomat. He was the first president of the Palestinian National Authority. While some people believe that he was born in Cairo, he called himself a son of Jerusalem.

Yasser Arafat, also known as Mohammed Yasser Abdel Rahman Abdel Raouf Arafat al-Qudwa, was born on August 24, 1929 in

Cairo. Yasser's father, Abdel Raouf al-Qudwa al-Husseini, was a famous textile merchant originally from Egypt. In 1933, Yasser's mother died of a kidney ailment. His father sent him and his younger brother to Jerusalem with their maternal uncle. In 1937, Arafat came back to Cairo.

During his school days, Arafat used to spend most of his holidays in Jerusalem. He developed a bond with the city. While living in Cairo, he would visit Jewish colonies against his father's will. However, Arafat never stopped admiring Jewish religion and their customs. In 1944, Arafat entered the University of King Fuad I. During his college days, he studied the works of Zionist scholars like Theodor Herzi. During this period, he also joined the Federation of Palestine and the Egyptian Union of Students. Later, he started his own magazine called *The Voice of Palestine.*

In 1952, Arafat was elected as the president of the General Union of Palestinian Students, a position he held till 1956. In the same year, he completed his civil engineering degree.

Later that year, when the Suez Crisis erupted, he was a part of the Egyptian army warring against Israel, United Kingdom and France.

For a brief period, he worked as a civil engineer in Egypt before shifting to Kuwait. In Kuwait, Arafat was employed in the department of public works. Later, he opened his own firm and kept contributing profits to the Palestinian cause. In 1958, Arafat found a new Palestinian national liberation movement called 'Fatah'. Around 1962, Arafat moved to Syria to recruit soldiers for an attack on Israel.

While the Arab countries were setting up an umbrella organization called the Palestine Liberal Organization, Arafat was busy setting up camps all along the Jordan-Israel border. Finally, he carried out his first armed operation on December 31, 1964. After the attack, Arafat was known internationally. He was on the cover page of *Time* magazine in the December 1968 issue.

On February 4, 1969, he was elected as the chairman of the PLO (Palestine Liberation

Organization). He had to work closely with other constituents, like the Popular Front for the Liberation of Palestine, and the Democratic Front for the Liberation of Palestine.

During 1987, the protest movement that continued for the next five years directed the world's attention to the plight of the Palestinians of Israel. Arafat then changed his policies and negotiated with the Israelis.

In December 1988, the PLO, under Arafat's leadership, recognized UN General Assembly Resolution 181, a plan to partition British Palestine. Concurrently, Arafat announced the establishment of an independent Palestinian state, and was declared the president of the new state. Later, 25 countries extended their support to the government-in-exile.

In 1993, PLO Chairman Yasser Arafat and Israeli Prime Minister Rabin signed the famous Oslo Accord. According to the accord, Palestinian self-rule was to be implemented in the Gaza strip and West Bank by removing Israeli settlements from the areas for a five-year period.

As Arafat worked in the above-mentioned areas, his task became strenuous, especially after the assassination of Prime Minister Rabin. Yet, Arafat kept working for the people till his last breath. In 1994, for establishing peace in the Middle East, Arafat, along with Yitzhak Rabin and Shimon Peres, received the Nobel Peace Prize.

In 1970, Arafat got married, at 61, to Suha Daoud Tawil. The couple had a son.

Arafat died at the age of 75, on November 11, 2004, because of a massive hemorrhagic cerebrovascular accident. His body, wrapped in the Palestinian flag, was sent to Cairo. He was buried in Ramallah in Cairo.

QUESTIONS

Q.1. Which president of America abolished the practice of slavery in the country?

Q.2. Che Guevera worked extremely hard as the minister for industries. What other important post did he volunteer for?

Q.3. Name two books by Charles de Gaulle.

Q.4. Which country was the first communist state in the Western hemisphere?

Q.5. Che Guevara was born in which country?

Q.6. Which leader is referred to as the 'Architect of Modern India'?

Q.7. The speech "I have a dream" was given by which influential leader?

Q.8. Which leader of the INC wanted Mahatma Gandhi to come back from South Africa and join India's struggle for independence?

Q.9. What military rank did Charles de Gaulle hold when France was invaded in 1940?

Q.10. Which preparatory school did Winston Churchill attend?

Q.11. Who earned the name Honest Abe?

Q.12. Whose leadership made a great impact on Deng Xiaoping?

Q.13. Who assassinated Abraham Lincoln?

Q.14. Who was the 44th president of the United States?

Q.15. In 1959, Yasser Arafat forged which organization?

Q.16. Who played a significant part in the Cuban Revolution?

Q.17. In which year was Gamal Abdel Nasser elected president?

Q.18. Who preceded Franklin Roosevelt as the US president?

Q.19. Which African city did Nelson Mandela live in?

Q.20. In 1967, Gamal Abdel Nasser resigned due to which reason?

Q.21. Where did Franklin Roosevelt attend college and graduate from in 1903?

Q.22. Barack Obama ran against which Republican candidate in the 2008 general election?

Q.23. When did Lee Kuan Yew publish *The Singapore Story*?

Q.24. Thomas Jefferson died on which anniversary of the Declaration of Independence?

Q.25. When did Lee Kuan Yew die?

Q.26. Why was Maximilien Robespierre eventually overthrown?

Q.27. In what year did Josip Broz Tito become president of Yugoslavia?

Q.28. Who did Nelson Mandela live with when his father died?

Q.29. What degree did Mikhail Gorbachev earn at Moscow University?

Q.30. In which army did Josip Broz Tito serve as sergeant-major?